The OKR Coach Handbook

A practical guide to setting up & running OKRs

By

By Roger Longden

Founder, There be Giants

Dedication

To team TBG, for always having my back as much as I have yours.

To Jake & Mollie, for always making me smile, despite the muddy paws and snoring.

Acknowledgement

We learn and grow by standing on the shoulders of giants. While that's exactly what I'd like to help you do with this Handbook, this is also an opportunity for me to make mention to a few of the Giants who have very generously lent me their shoulders along the way.

I want to start by thanking Brett Knowles of PM2 Consulting. While Brett likes to give off a somewhat hard-faced persona, he is one of the most generous people I have met in the business. I was lucky enough to be inducted into the ways of OKRs by him, and he provided me with a significant springboard in the shape of his knowledge, expertise and support. There be Giants would not be in the position it is today if it wasn't for the help Brett has offered along the way.

Secondly, I want to thank my old business partner Nick Robinson. Nick challenged me to find my "soapbox" - the thing that I could get really passionate about because it bugged the heck out of me! That was Performance Management, and my research on that led me to OKRs.

Thirdly, I'd like to thank our clients around the world for allowing myself and the team to work on some fantastic projects, each one being a learning experience that helps us to continually evolve how we work.

Finally, I'd like to thank all in Team TBG. I'm hugely proud of how you have all stepped up over the challenging times since C-19 took hold. It feels like we're tighter now than we have ever been, and I couldn't have created this book without your daily support.

Oh, and I want to thank my dogs and my Godsons for being my sorely needed distractions during Covid-19; you've both kept me balanced.

About the Author

Originally working as a Performance Coach following a career in IT infrastructure, Roger shifted his focus to OKRs back in 2015. Since then, he has built up There be Giants into the international consultancy it is today. Known for their OKR expertise, he and his teams now work with clients from North & South America, Africa, Europe, Asia and Aus & NZ, helping them to become world-class in how they inspire their organisations to align with their strategy.

Contents

Introduction

By all means, please make use of this Handbook by itself. I'm sure if you're new to OKRs and are thinking, "how the heck do I do them?" then you'll gain a lot from it. However, it has also been written as a physical takeaway for those studying on one of our courses in the OKR Coach Academy (www.okrcoach.academy)

I regard OKRs not as a model to get wrong or right but as a collection of principles and practices which can be interpreted and applied in many different ways. The TBG OKR methodology is just such an interpretation, and it is what this Handbook is based on. This means it's not a "bible" as such, so you're not getting OKRs wrong if you don't adhere to it by the letter. It is merely offered as a starting point or an indication of what we have found to work well over our years of working with OKRs. In fact, central to our methodology is the principle of reflective practice, which positively encourages the constant iteration and improvement of your OKR practice, so we fully expect you not to be following our method by the book once you're well underway with OKRs.

Fundamentally, I've written this Handbook to both be practical and also to be a way of bringing to life the underlying principles of OKRs, these being:

- Transparency
- Accountability
- Alignment

- Empowerment
- Agility

So, while I encourage you to evolve and adapt from the practices shared in this Handbook, I also urge you not to lose sight of these principles as if you do stray from them, then that is when you're likely to be "getting OKRs wrong."

I'm also assuming that you are reading this Handbook either already with a degree of coaching ability or that you are part of a cohort in our OKR Coach Academy where you will build up your coaching skills. The questions you choose and the way you ask them are an essential part of being an OKR Coach; it's not ALL about just writing OKRs!

One final point to mention; for those who are not part of a cohort in our OKR Coach Academy, it will be beneficial for you to work through our OKR Activator e-learning program, which provides essential OKR foundational knowledge. Again, you can access this via: www.okrcoach.academy.

I wish you all the best in your OKR adventures!

Roger
Founder - There be Giants
roger@therebegiants.com

Set-Up

The first of the two sections within the Handbook, Set-up, takes you through how to help a client/organisation/team build up their OKRs. It pays to invest time in doing this. It's when alignment starts to build, empowerment can be practised, and transparency and accountability begin to form.

Point of Clarity

Throughout this Handbook, I refer to 12-month and 3-month OKRs. These timeframes are not set in stone. I use them to distinguish between OKRs, which run for a more extended period and are used for providing clarity and direction for the wider business and OKRs, which run for a short period and are more tactical in nature.

While I find that 12-month OKRs are often the norm, there may be justification to flex them. E.g. if you're starting OKRs and you're not at the beginning of a year, you may decide to extend your first 12-month OKRs to, say, 15 months.

More often, I see variations at the tactical level, as their timeframe should be driven by the "drumbeat" of your business/organisation. I've known larger organisations and public sector bodies opt for 4-month OKR cycles as this gave them longer to work on them, and they felt three cycles per year were sufficient. Three months, however, is by far the most common timeframe. The important point is to choose a timeframe and get going; there is nothing stopping you from changing it at a later date.

Translating Strategy into 12-Month OKRs

In this first section, I walk you through how to build a set of OKRs based on a strategy that already exists. This is a crucial point to note as this method is not designed to help develop strategy; there are plenty of toolsets out there to help you do that. So, if a clear strategy doesn't exist, then one is needed before this process can start.

Framing Strategy And Identifying Priorities

The business'/organisation's vision, mission and strategy should be its "north star."

This means that everything it does should be in pursuit of it, and if not, then questions should be asked to check if the activity is worth doing or if the strategy is still fit-for-purpose. OKRs are the translation of strategy into the day-to-day and the week-by-week. Without them, too much is left to best judgement and interpretation, which can vary widely.

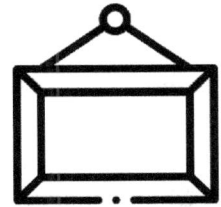

Also, vision and strategy are the domain of senior executives. They live and breathe it, and while that's a large part of their role, they are also leaders, and leaders need to be good communicators. What we often see is a blind spot around vision and strategy - e.g. the Execs get it and so, therefore, assume so does everyone else. The reality is, they don't.

You will shortly be introduced to the Strategy Frame. Working through it builds up a single-page summary of the vital elements within their game plan. No sifting through weighty documents, no trying to understand complex corporate jargon. Just an easy-to-understand framing of what matters most.

Oh, and you can use this step (or parts of it) with any team, not just an Executive team.

Meet: Big Moves

A large shift is needed to move from where you are now to where you want to be in the future. It's not an objective; it sits at a higher level. You might have heard them called "strategic themes" or "strategic pillars" (TBG even worked with a client who liked to call them "Anchors").

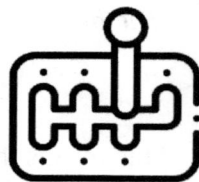

The truth is, I'm not precious what you call them; I just like 'Big Move' as it suggests there's some purposeful action involved!

Purpose, Impact & Way

Think of the Big Moves as the high-level "way" in which they will achieve their "impact" (their Mission) and the OKRs which you're going to help them build as the next level of detail to their "way".

So what does a Strategy Frame look like?

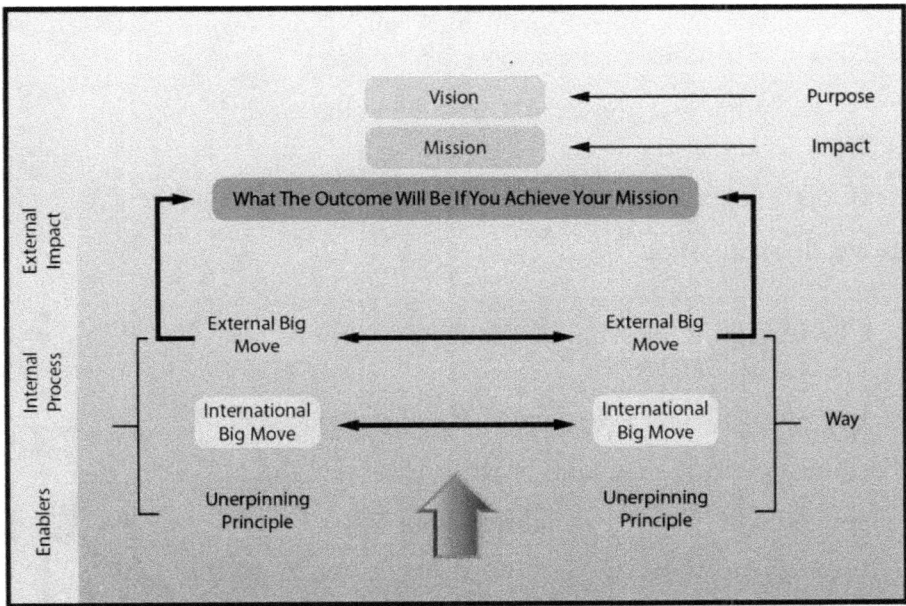

Adapted from Knowles 2019

It's your job to help the team you're working with fill in the blanks, not to do them for them

Clarifying the Vision (Purpose)

Remember, this is a statement that should be future-based and is meant to give inspiration and direction to those reading it. Think purpose.

They don't need something which reads like a 5-year objective; this should be a high-level statement that has a bit of punch and aspiration in it.

Questions to help clarify the Vision:

- What's the timescale? (3-5 years)
- Why does the business exist?
- What is it you want to change in the world?

If a Vision statement already exists, then challenge them to test it against these questions

Clarifying the Mission (Impact)

Whereas a Vision statement is about purpose, a Mission statement is about broadly defining the impact you will have if you achieve your Vision.

It's possible they might start to see some measures come in at this point; this is what is noted in the "outcome" box.

Questions to help clarify the Mission:

- What evidence will you see?
- How will you know you've achieved all you want to accomplish by then?
- What will be different?

If a mission statement exists, challenge them to test it against these questions.

As with the Vision statement, if this needs further work, just make sure that someone owns seeing this is done and set a deadline for it to be completed.

The Big Moves (Way)

Here's where you might have to start helping to build more than clarify. As said earlier, Big Moves are the broad shifts that need to happen if the organisation is to move from where it is now to where it wants to be.

It's OK for these to be reasonably broad terms like "customer-centric" or "people capability", and it's best not to go more than 3 at each level.

Big Moves are designed to help lead teams into a more specific objective setting.

A question to help build Big Moves:

> Thinking about where you are currently, what are the areas you need to focus on to help you achieve your Vision & Mission? (Encourage them to consider this from the 3 perspectives on the left of the Frame)

External Impact - the shifts you need to make concerning Clients and Markets - e.g. new sectors, new geographies

Internal Processes - the shifts you need to make internally if you're to achieve your External Big Moves - e.g. develop a new product, invest in new systems, develop capability

Enablers - what you will need & rely on to help you in making these shifts. e.g. your values, guiding principles, house rules, standards, investment

The Next Step

Building up the Strategy Frame is the next step as they select their vital 3 for each level. Below is an example of a Strategy Frame for a fictional tech business (something like FitBit).

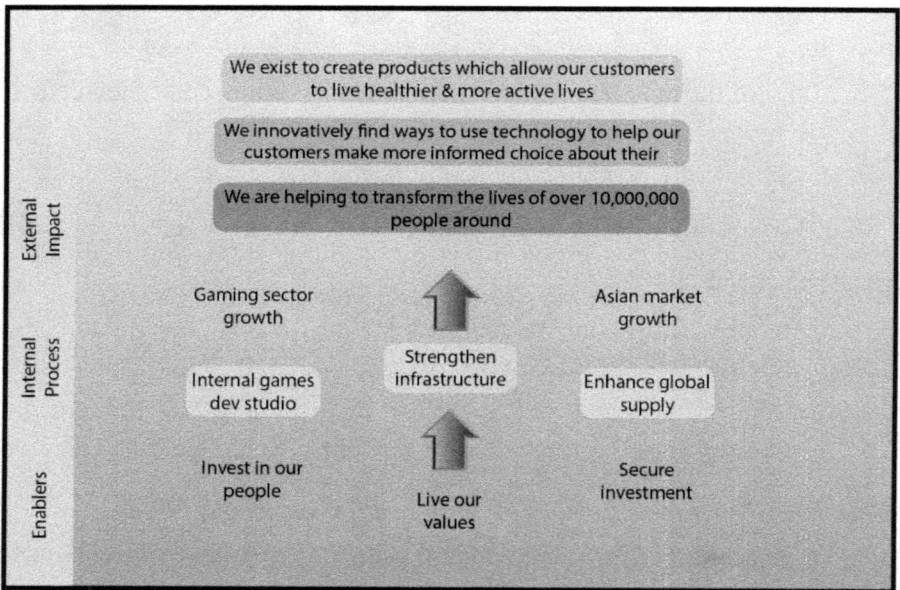

Prioritisation

This is always a challenge as pretty much most Executive teams will want it all! However, clarity is a crucial principle of OKRs, and this is where we can start to build that focus. If it doesn't, then there's no way it will appear anywhere else.

Try giving them 100 points to allocate to their Big Moves/Principles to help define their priorities for the next 12 months(it's cheating to distribute them equally across everything!)

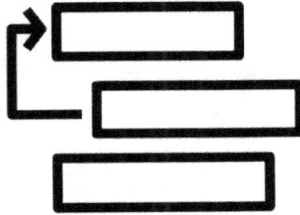

What a finished Strategy Frame looks like

(Now, with added prioritisation examples!)

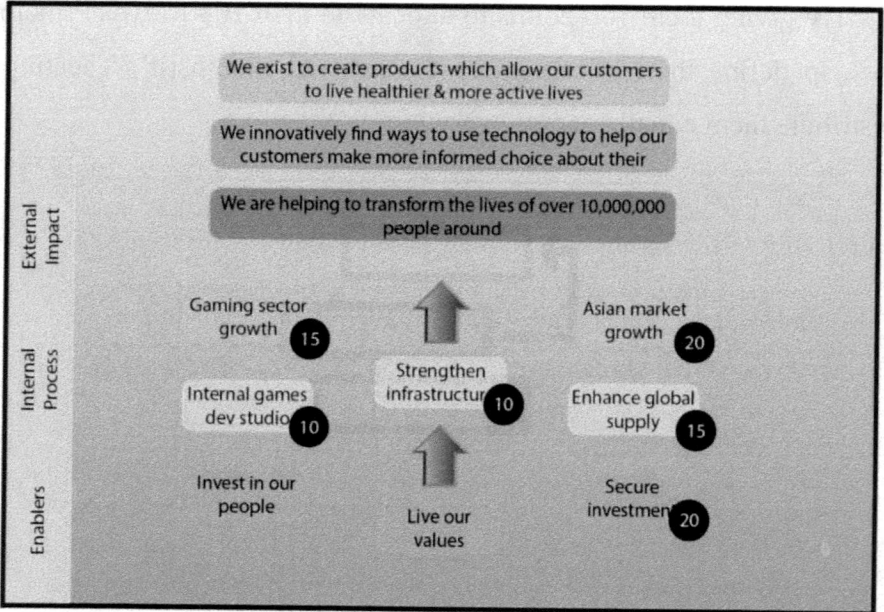

The final step is to help the team to select their "chosen few" so they are genuinely prioritising. In the example below, I'd suggest setting a cut off at 15 points, so they have 4 to work with, as 7 is too many. It's not to say that the others need to be completely dropped; it might be possible to integrate them into the selected priorities. For e.g. from the example below, the "wearable tech sector" could be a sub-component of "Asian market growth."

Don't underestimate how long this work can take. We give at least a day to work on this with an Executive team, and it's entirely possible that it might need a few iterations before they are happy with it.

Also, remember you can use this step (or parts of it) to work through vision/mission work with any team, not just an Executive team.

Building 12-month Objectives & Identifying Key Contributors

12-month OKRs act as the critical link between strategic priorities and what teams need to be focussing on to achieve the outcomes the business/organisation is seeking.

View them as a clear presentation of the business'/organisation's strategy in a way that everyone, at all levels, can understand. They cut through the "waffle" which strategic planning documents can often contain, thereby making the essential clear and visible. They are the spotlight that helps everyone to see what will drive the greatest value over the year ahead.

I also deliberately don't include Key Results at this stage. I find it helps keep thinking clear. Including Key Results at this point would require thinking at both strategic and detailed levels, and these are different mindsets.

Also, the Exec/C-level team may be inviting in Key Contributors to help form the Key Results, and they need to work out who they are first.

Break out the post-its

What you need first are ideas, and those should be in answer to the question:

"What do we need to work on over the next year to help us achieve our Big Moves?"

This is deliberately a very open question as you want to be opening up thinking, not narrowing it down. If they write their ideas down on post-its, it makes it easier to work large scale on a big wall. This helps people to make connections and see the whole picture.

Again, don't rush this. A typical Exec team will have lots of opinions, and so they need the chance to work through the suggestions and ideas.

Is there a desire to use OKRs to help encourage innovation?

If so, then it really is worth encouraging the team to generate some new thinking. This is the time for the outlying ideas.

Perhaps try asking them what they might like to test?

Narrowing Down

Don't forget: focus comes from having only a vital few

The next step is to help them zero in on the ideas which will have the greatest impact on the prioritised Big Moves. You can start this by grouping all the ideas around the specific Big Moves that they would help to achieve (some ideas might support more than one Big Move). This helps to build a picture of the groups thinking so far. If the same idea has come up more than once, then it's worthy of further discussion and debate; just make sure that you are providing sufficient challenge to check that group-think isn't the influence here; your aim is to make sure individual contributions are explored and discussed.

Questions such as these will help:

- Why this idea?
- How do you see it having an impact on the Big Move?
- What timeframe would be needed to achieve it?
- Do any of the other ideas overlap/contribute to it?

Ideally, you are aiming for one idea per Big Move to make the cut. There is possibly justification for having more than one if the Big Move achieves a very high weighting. 3 is the ideal number, but definitely no more than 5 in total.

Drafting the 12-month Objectives

Before you start - it's worth taking stock of the time you have left and maybe linking the next step up as homework.

Now they know the chosen ideas/suggestions/project/initiatives for each prioritised Big Move, the group can have a go at drafting up some powerful Objective statements. It's useful to agree on initial owners at this stage, so it's clear who will be drafting the objective (they might not be the owner once it's live, though).

They need to know what a powerful Objective statement looks like first, though! If you have completed our OKR Activator course, then you can draw on your learning from that to coach them. Or, you can obtain access to either Activator or just OKR writing training for them to complete in advance as e-learning. Just drop a note to growth@therebegiants.com, and we'll arrange this for you.

Once all the drafts are in, the team needs to review and agree on the chosen ones, which can then feed into the next step, but first, they need testing...

Meet Yoda

If you've completed OKR Activator, you will have been introduced to the "Alien test." We often find an Exec team has a blind spot in the language and terms they use. They live and breathe strategy, so it's easy for them to assume that everyone else gets it too.

They don't.

Remember to put all Objectives through the "alien test" by asking:

"If Yoda arrived tomorrow and read your Objective, would it make sense to him?"

BEWARE - Potential Trap Lies Ahead!

Now you have helped them create their 12-month Objectives, the temptation is often to look to all the Heads of Functions to see what their OKRs should be.

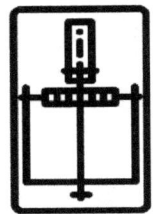

DON'T

We're not saying Functions don't have a role to play, but jumping straight into that question leads to a set of Functional OKRs that will reinforce silo-working.

This means Functions end up focussing on their own Objectives rather than working on shared ones which encourage collaboration and agility and ultimately focus on strategic priorities rather than hierarchical norms.

Before we show you how to avoid this, let's just take a look at what a well-structured team OKR looks like

	Owned by
Objective: Smash open Asia so that we are less dependent on our home market	Objective Lead
Key Result I: Revenue generated from sales in Asia has grown from 5% to 30%	Key Contributor A
Key Result 2: Our lead to sales conversation ratio stands at 4:1 (currently 10:1)	Key Contributor B
Key Result 3: We constantly generate at least 5000 leads per quarter	Key Contributor C

The key point to note here is that it is entirely possible for the Objective to be owned by one person (the Objective Lead) and the Key Results by other people (the Key Contributors). This naturally helps a small team to form to focus on their shared objective for as long as it runs.

Objective Lead - provides leadership for the contributors, ensuring they have the clarity, support and resources needed to achieve the Key Results.

Key Contributor - brings specialist knowledge to the team. May represent the area they are part of, which, in turn, supports them in achieving the KR.

You need to guide the Exec team in working out who those Key Contributors should be so that they can be invited to join for the next step, so that's what we will cover next.

Thinking cross-functionally and identifying Key Contributors

Start by asking the team:

"What are the Core Activities in the business/organisation?"

"Core Activities" can be functions, but they can also be tribes, squads, value-creation streams, project teams, etc. You're trying to get them thinking outside normal Functional boundaries.

Once you have the Core Activities identified, work through each of the 12-month Objectives and ask:

"What level of contribution does each Core Activity need to make to each Objective?"

The outcome you're aiming for is a list of Core Activities for each Objective from which Key Contributors should be invited to join the process from the next step onwards.

The final step is for invitations to go out to Key Contributors to join from the next step.

Building 12-Month Key Results

Objectives alone are a bit useless. In fact, they are just aspirations.

Key Results are what give OKRs the edge. They help you to understand what you're aiming to achieve and how you will know if you hit it, minus the assumption, ambiguity or bias.

We set them at this level because it's essential to understand how all the 3-month activity is contributing to the broader business goals. This means that regularly (probably quarterly), they can be updated once the previous 3 months' results are understood. The gap that's left can then help inform the focus of the following 3 months' OKRs.

Important Pre-Work

It's assumed that all participants have been trained on how to write great Key Results, either by completing OKR Activator or OKR Skills (which just contains the Objective and Key Result modules from OKR Activator). If not, then you need to train them in the main points from the modules so they will be able to form the right Key Results.

If you need access to these, then head over to www.okrcoach.academy

It's post-it time again!

Before you start writing new ones, however, it's worth making time for the Exec to run through the 12-month Objectives with the new Key Contributors who

are now around the table and for the Exec to explain why they have been invited to join from this point onwards.

Once everyone is up to speed with the 12-month objectives, it's time to start exploring some critical questions for each Objective, such as:

"What would be a great outcome for this?"

"How would we know we've achieved it?"

"What's the evidence we will see?"

You could break them into small groups, which each take an Objective and then ask them to note their responses to the questions on post-its.

Drafting the Key Results

Let's just have a quick recap.

Writing a Key Result can be a bit trickier than an Objective, so it's worth offering these best-practice reminders:

- All KRs need a metric that should show the starting point and the result being aimed for
- The strongest KRs focus on OUTCOME, not action (i.e. they measure the result of an action, not the completion of the action itself)
- No "binary" (i.e. we do/don't achieve X) KRs should be allowed. If any are drafted, then look at how they could be written as percentage milestones so progress can be reported

With these fresh in their minds, now is the point to ask them to draft their Key Results. Remember, it's the outcome, not the action we're looking for here, so if their KRs read like a big to-do list, then more work is needed.

As a guideline, 3 per Objective is a good number, too many, and it becomes confusing and unclear what the focus really is.

Oh, and it's common for teams to get hung up on what the actual numbers should be at this point. Encourage them to not dive into the specifics at this point, for draft KRs "from X to Y" does the job, and the blanks can be filled in as homework.

What you are looking for

When the groups have had a go at drafting their Key Results, it's a good idea to bring everyone back together for a critique. This is a great opportunity to introduce some coaching into the process.

Try asking each group to share what they have drafted and ask the others for feedback on how well it measures up against the best practice.

This is also a chance for them to judge if it needs to be a committed or aspirational Key Result, and if it's aspirational, does it have sufficient stretch in it?

Time to build commitment

You should now be at the point where they have a reasonably well-formed set of Key Results, so there are a few things left to do:

- Each Key Result needs an owner, as accountability won't happen without them.
- Decide if each Key Result is either "aspirational" or "committed."
- If data needs to be confirmed to finalise a metric, then gain commitment from the KR owner that they will do this.
- Key Contributors need to decide who from their areas they need to invite into the forming of the 3-month OKRs.

Forming 3-Month OKRs

Building The 3-Month Objectives

We very often are asked if the 12-month Key Result can be the Objective at the next level?

The simple answer is no, not if you want your OKRs to work as they should. Besides, Objective statements shouldn't have any metrics in them; what a 3-month Objective should do is "chunk down" the 12 month one into something more meaningful for the team who will be working with it.

Remember, an Objective should motivate and, dare we say, even inspire. That means it has to be relevant to the team who is working with it.

With that aim in mind, it's a valuable activity to allow whatever team might be coming together to work on an OKR to draft their own. This is exactly how you build more empowerment and alignment and encourage collaboration.

Also, remember that these teams are very likely to be cross-functional, so some of the people in the room (or online) might be working together for the first time.

Now is the time to lay out the road ahead

Before diving into 3-month Objectives, given there are likely new people in the room, it's essential that the Leads who each own a 12-month OKR talk through what's been created so far.

Doing this builds alignment and helps to set the "parameters" for the work ahead.

Once everyone is at the same point, then work on the 3-month Objectives can start, but before you do, just help the new joiners out by showing them the type of structure they are aiming for in their OKRs.

You could even use this opportunity to test out what those working on the 12-month OKRs remember rather than jumping straight into training them!

Follow these steps to help build up and refine the 3-month Objectives

1. Form Groups

Now everyone understands the 12-month OKRs, it's time for people to form into the natural groups which will work on drafting the supporting 3-month Objectives.

2. Build & select ideas

Once they are in groups, they should start to (with good old post-its) work up their ideas. Try putting this question to them to guide their thinking:

"What is it we need to work on or achieve over the next 3 months to have an impact on our 12-month OKRs?"

If you have some people who are less likely to share and speak up than others, then ask them to each individually note down their ideas before they discuss them as a group. They can then see how many similar ideas there are, which is a good indicator of what the right choice(s) might be.

They need to narrow it down to 2-3 ideas per 12-month OKR.

3. Share ideas

Once they have their 2-3 ideas, bring them back together as a full group and facilitate sharing. This gives the opportunity to see what else is being suggested and receive feedback on their ideas. Help them spot any overlaps/duplications and any dependencies.

4. Refine & draft Objective statements

Back in their smaller groups and taking what came out of the wider sharing, they now need to refine their ideas and have a go at drafting their Objective statements. Before they start, check in with them on the qualities which make a great Objective statement and test their recall, don't just list them for them!

27

5. Agree on Objective statements

Once they have drafted their statements, it's time to come back together and for someone to present their group so they can receive feedback/critique to help refine it.

It is worthwhile giving thought to resourcing at this point. Do the areas which need to contribute have the bandwidth and resources to do so? If not, what can be done to find that resource to free up capacity to contribute to the OKR?

You're aiming to get them to the point of an agreement by this stage and a Lead to own each Objective.

It's quite normal for this step in the process to take at least half a day and possibly a full day, depending on the number of people involved and the number of OKRs being aligned into.

Common Questions At This Point

What if an Objective needs longer than 3 months?

Quite common. Write the Objective as usual. The Key Results will frame where you need to be by the end of 3 months.

What if we think of an Objective that can't start yet?

Capture it and park it. If you're using a system, put it in but leave it in draft form for now.

How many Objectives should we have?

2-3 per 12-month Objective is about right. 1 is fine too, but no more than 3, as that's likely to dilute the focus.

Suggested Homework

In prep for the next workshop, ask participants to:

1. Make sure they have completed their Key Result e-learning (if applicable)
2. Come ready with some ideas for Key Results for their Objectives.

Building 3-month Key Results

A blunt nail has no point, and neither does an Objective without its Key Results

Measurement is vital. For some, it could be a bit scary at first if it's a new practice (and it is in more businesses/organisations than you'd think). This is often because measurement has been a tool to help blame and beat others up for falling short, so it's often been safer not to measure at all.

This is why "Psychological Safety" is vital for OKRs to work well. If you have completed our OKR Activator course, you will have had an introduction to the principles of Psychological Safety, and if you are working with us to gain your OKR Coach qualification, then you will cover it in more detail.

3-month Key Results become the point of focus for reflection, reporting and check-ins throughout the quarter. They are critical for transparency, so progress and confidence levels can be tracked without ambiguity and guesswork.

Important Pre-Work

It's assumed that all participants have been trained on how to write great Key Results, either by completing OKR Activator or OKR Skills (which just contains the Objective and Key Result modules from OKR Activator). If not, then you need to train them in the main points from the modules so they will be able to form the right Key Results.

It's post-it time again

Everyone must be at the same starting point so take some time to revisit the 3-month Objectives drafted, especially if they took a homework task to refine them further.

Pro tip:

Whenever Objectives or Key Results are being presented back, use that as an opportunity to ask those listening to provide feedback and critique so you can see their level of understanding and coach them as necessary.

Once everyone is up to speed with the 3-month objectives, it's time to start work on their Key Results. Ask them to form back into their small groups and use these questions to prompt their thinking:

- "What would be a great outcome for this?"
- "How would we know we've achieved it?"
- "What's the evidence we will see?"

Before you start, however, you might want to run a quick drafting Key Results refresh with them. Again, this is an opportunity to test their knowledge as they should have picked up the main points from the e-learning.

This is a pretty similar step to the one you followed for the 12-month Key Results.

Bring them back together and encourage each group to share what they have drafted and ask the others to offer feedback on how well it measures up to best practice.

This is also a chance for them to judge if it needs to be a committed or aspirational Key Result, and if it's aspirational, does it have sufficient stretch in it?

The Home Stretch

You should now be at the point where all the groups have a reasonably well-formed set of Key Results, so there are a few things left to check:

1. Each Key Result needs an owner, as accountability won't happen without them.
2. Decide if each Key Result is either "aspirational" or "committed."
3. If data needs to be confirmed to finalise a metric, then gain commitment from the KR owner that they will do this.
4. Key Contributors need to decide who from their areas they need to invite into the forming of the 3-month OKRs if the 3rd level of OKRs is to be used.

Any loose ends should be tied up before moving on to the final "ceremony" before the OKRs go live: the Show & Tell.

Running the Cycle

OK, so by now, OKRs should be feeling a bit different to any previous objective setting that people have been involved in before. That's not enough, though. If you do the work you've done and decide to leave it there, then OKRs will fail. "Set & forget" is the enemy of OKRs, and it's the routines that make them genuinely different to traditional management-by-objective activity.

High-performance is a habit, not a fluke. I've seen it in both business and in the coaching I used to do at an elite level in rowing. The individuals and teams who are high-achieving are those who routinely test/learn/adapt. This is what leads to incremental improvement. The cyclical nature of OKRs provides the perfect opportunity for this.

These are the reasons why I have provided an outline for the critical "ceremonies" within an OKR cycle. Again, these are a blueprint, not a set of rules, so by all means, use them as a starting point and then adapt as you progress through your cycles.

Show & Tells

If OKRs were to go live as soon as they had been created by the teams working on them, then you'd be missing out on one of the most significant contributors to alignment. We've yet to meet an organisation using OKRs that didn't want to build alignment!

The purpose of the Show & Tell is to bring together all those who will be working on the OKRs for the next period, so everyone has the chance to see and hear how they "fit" together. Think of it as viewing the OKR landscape for the next period.

This is the chance for OKR Leads & Contributors to talk through what they have created.

It's then down to everyone else to probe, ask questions and understand what's behind the OKRs and the context behind them.

This conversation needs to bring to the surface any dependencies and risks which have not yet been discussed so agreements can be reached.

The endpoint of the Show & Tell is to gain the thumbs up from everyone and ensure their commitment to the OKRs for the period ahead.

Recommended Structure

Overlaps & Gaps

Everyone sharing the OKRs they have drafted allows for the identification and exploration of any duplication (overlaps) and anything which might have been overlooked (gaps). These can then be discussed, and an agreement reached on how they will be managed.

Risks & Dependencies

All risks and dependencies should also be captured, discussed, and actions agreed on how to mitigate or avoid them. This often is managed by having the right contributors on the OKR teams.

Alignment & Commitment

The Show & Tell is the final step in forging alignment across the teams and in gaining commitment from all present to progress with the OKRs for the period ahead.

Kick off with Some Ground Rules

The Show & Tell needs to be an open, honest and respectful conversation in which people feel comfortable speaking up and challenging if necessary. People need to feel safe enough to do this, and it's entirely possible some might not, especially if you have a mix of seniority in the room.

Agreeing on a set of ground rules with everyone present will help establish some psychological safety.

- Anyone can challenge anyone without reprise.
- No idea is a stupid idea.
- We all agree to listen when someone speaks up.

Tell The Story

These are the steps we recommend you follow when facilitating the Show & Tell:

1. Present the Objective

This is for the Objective Lead to do. Guide them in covering: An outline of the Objective

The "parent" OKR(s) it aligns into

The shared purpose behind it - why it's worth doing & its benefit/impact

2. Talk through Key Results

This is for either the Objective Lead or the Key Contributors to talk through. Guide them in covering:

How they believe the Key Results will be evidence of impact

Why the Key Results are the right ones for what needs to be measured

It's crucial to "test" the Key Results at this stage to be certain that they are a good measure of the outcome the Objective is aiming for.

3. Risks & Dependencies

Keeping with the Objective Lead, guide them in outlining the risk and dependencies which have been identified for their Objective.

With the risks, encourage them to share how they will be mitigated or avoided.

With the dependencies, check with the other parties to ensure they understand it, accept it and commit to supporting it.

If anything needs to be taken away for further discussion, then capture this and support it being followed through.

4. Team

The conversation so far should now give you a good sense of if the right people are on the OKR team.

Is the Lead the right one?

Are the Key Contributors the right ones?

If not, then agree with the OKR team who is and how they will be invited onto the team.

It's a good idea to round off by checking in on:

Is any further clarity needed?

Has anything been overlooked?

Who else do the OKRs need to be shared with, and how will this happen?

The full picture of the OKR "landscape" should be clear now, so it's time to check that all gaps and overlaps have been resolved?

Is Everyone Happy?

With all OKRs covered in the way we have recommended, you will be at the point where you can ask if everyone is ready to commit.

There may be some uncertainty, there may be some nervousness around stretch, and there may be some concern around possible failure, but that should all be OK.

There's no guarantee with OKRs, just collaboration, support and alignment. If there was a guarantee, then they probably are not stretching enough. 😁

As the quarter progresses, that's when teams can track and report on their confidence levels so they can flag early on if there's an issue.

Check-Ins

Quite simply, OKRs without check-ins are pretty pointless. The OKRs end up as set-and-forget and lose impact, influence and credibility.

One of the biggest challenges OKRs face at introduction is the often negative associations with the term "objective." It is frequently linked to performance management and individual annual objectives, which have had a bad rep for many years now as being unfair and ineffective.

Therefore, it's vital that OKRs "feel" different from any other past use of objectives. Check-ins are a way to achieve this.

Check-ins are a well-proven practice of Agile, and it's no error that they feature in OKR best practice. A brief (30min max) team check-in every week or two weeks anchors the team and keeps priorities front-and-centre for them. This helps in daily decision making on where to focus time, energy and resources.

Also, in preparation for the check-in, each team member should be updating their progress and confidence scores. Assuming these are entered into a system, the data then becomes visible to all. This means Leadership can take their high-level view without the need for additional reporting and be confident they are seeing the latest data. It also means the check-in itself can be run using the system to view the data, rather than adding extra work, such as producing slide packs.

Teams Might Need Convincing at First

Remember, check-ins could be a new concept to many people.

Teams need to be on-side if they are to try running check-ins. Below are the typical concerns we hear.

We don't know how to run them.

That's why you're here! A vital job for the OKR Coach is to train/guide/support teams in running great check-ins. So remind the teams they are not alone on this journey!

It's yet another meeting we now need to do

It's not about adding more on top; help the team to find a regular meeting they already have and adapt that. This is not a new activity - it's just being done in a different way.

It's just going to be a chance for us to be kicked.

This is about the level of safety people feel to challenge and speak up. It's vital this is high. If you decide to train as an OKR Coach with us, you will have the chance to learn more about how to build up Psychological safety, which is vital for effective OKR conversations.

So Those Are The Concerns, But What About The Benefits?

Maintains momentum

It's easy to be pulled off course; plenty of distractions. Having a regular OKR check-in keeps the team on track.

Focus is on results, not actions

Check-ins are for focussing on what's been achieved, not actions taken. This makes them far more focused.

Transparency made real

Both the discussion and the system updates help everyone understand OKR's progress.

Accountability is clear

Having to regularly discuss updates in a team check-in brings with it broader accountability, more so than if they were just discussed between manager and team member.

Time-efficient

The structure and focus of a check-in mean it shouldn't be a long meeting - 30 minutes is ideal.

Lightens reporting workload

Because in preparation, team members log their updates in the system. The system can be used to report progress for anyone in the organisation. No additional slide packs required!

What Does A Good Check-In Look Like?

You don't want them to be like every other meeting.

It really helps if they can feel different. This will mainly come from how they are run. Below are some tips on how to give them a different feel to regular meetings:

Keep them short

Absolutely critical. Aim for no more than 30 minutes.

Don't let them turn into a talking shop

Keep the discussion focussed on results and solutions for issues/blockers, not work done.

Focus on exceptions first

Use the system data to guide the discussion. Low confidence & low progress should be top of the agenda.

Essential Preparation

If the check-in is to be brief and to the point, then team members need to prepare beforehand. They can do this by updating their Key Results on the system. This is vital because:

The team can review each other's updates before the meeting, so they come in already informed.

Their updates are not just visible to the team but also across the system so other stakeholders can see progress and confidence.

Suggested Structure

1. Start with the exceptions

By "exceptions", we mean things that might not be on track. There are 2 "flags" to focus on here:

Low confidence

High confidence/low progress

It should be down to the Key Result owner (Key Contributor) to talk through it. If it looks like a more extended conversation is needed, then park that for discussion after the check-in so that it does not overrun.

This is not an opportunity for blaming or telling off; it's important that questions such as "what can we all do to help achieve this?" are explored. There could be scope to share resources, or maybe the Objective Lead could escalate if the blocker is outside the team.

2. Move to the successes

It's important to give recognition for the great work done.

3. Run through the priorities for the next week/2 weeks

Each team member shares what they will be focussing on up to the next check-in.

Check-ins are not about proving how busy you've been!

Something to watch out for is that people often like to share all the things they have done, all the items they have ticked off. That's all well and good, but that's not for an OKR check-in for 2 reasons:

We only want to know the status of the Key Results.

We want to keep the check-in conversation as brief and focused as possible.

Being drawn into these types of conversations will mean the check-in takes much longer than it needs to!

Retrospectives

Alas, retrospectives don't directly increase sales. Still, if you want to see continuous improvement, rapid product development and lots of innovation, then there has to be learning. Much of that can come from the reflections in retrospectives.

Carol Dweck (Professor of Psychology at Stanford) has done a lot of work on Growth Mindset. She's identified that it can exist at both individual, team and organisational levels. It's a Growth Mindset that drives us to always look for new solutions, to not be blown off course by failure, but to seize the learning and build on it.

A Growth Mindset is essential if the organisation (and its leadership) are going to encourage the often overlooked but essential type of performance: adaptive performance.

Most organisations only focus on tactical performance (targets, budgets, etc.), but if you want true agility, then adaptive performance is vital. It is concerned with how well we recover from a setback, how we deal with change and how skilled we are at learning.

Organisations can build a strong Growth Mindset by rewarding learning as much as progress and also by putting emphasis on the processes which underpin these, as they ultimately lead to bottom-line impact.

You can read Dweck's HBR paper on Growth Mindset. Go to HBR.com and search for "Dweck Growth Mindset"

You can read McGregor & Doshi's HBR paper on the 2 types of performance. Go to HBR.com and search for "Doshi 2 types of performance."

What A Retro Should Seek To Do

A good Retro should stimulate reflection to learn from:

1. The results achieved over the last cycle and why
2. How OKRs have worked as a process and how we could gain even more from our use of them

These are 2 different perspectives. 1 is about learning from what happened within the content and focus of the specific OKRs. 2 is about taking a "birds-eye" view of the whole "process" of OKRs (not just the software system, but also the habits, routines etc.) to understand how it could be improved.

The learning to come out of these 2 perspectives can then be applied to the next year/quarter, so iterative improvements are made, and growth in knowledge, capability and performance happens.

Homework

It's a good idea to share the questions they will be working through in the Retro in advance so they can give thought and prepare their contributions.

Ask them to consider the following questions from both content and process perspectives:

What worked well?

This is about the way OKRs have been used. It's important to recognise the value they are adding and give recognition to those who are role modelling their use. This is a vital part of change management in the early stages of OKRs as it helps to embed the change when great examples of practice are recognised.

Where something has worked really well, a couple of great coaching questions to then ask are, "How can we build on this? How can we make sure that it's repeated?"

What could be better in the next quarter?

OK, so not everything is going to work the first time, and failure is actually an option (as long as the risk is sensible and managed!)

An open and honest conversation is needed here, without blame. As soon as blame appears, people will close down. They need to feel safe enough to talk about what's not going to plan, and that is where the most valuable learning (and growth potential) lies.

Try avoiding "why" as a question. This can often elicit a defensive response as it implies that the person responding has to justify themselves. Questions like "how can we approach this differently next time?" and "If we were to do this again, what would we do differently?" are good coaching ones to try here.

What is it we're doing but maybe don't need to?

Often overlooked but important to reflect on to make sure processes are kept as lean as possible and the time demand is no more than it needs to be.

Questions like "What is it we're doing which isn't adding much value?" and "What wouldn't we miss if we stopped doing it?" are good coaching questions to use at this point.

Preparation

Time to break out the post-its again!

If you're doing the session in a room with everyone, then choose a big wall and create a matrix by writing out post-its as follows:

Along the top row, write 5 post-its:

- Cadence
- Crafting
- System
- Culture
- Alignment

These are taken from our OKR skills model (the 6th is evolution, and you're doing that by running the Retro!) and provide a framework for reflection.

Down the left column, write 3 post-its:

- Well
- Better
- Not needed

These represent the questions they will be prompted to answer.

If you're running this session remotely, you can set these up on a shared Google doc that everyone has access to.

Recommended Structure

Aim for no more than 90 minutes

1. Outline the purpose and scope of the session

This is likely to be a once-a-quarter conversation, so it's worth just taking a pause to allow everyone to get comfortable with its unique nature.

It's worth reminding everyone that they all share the same desire to have an impact and that OKR is the way they are all trying to do that, so everyone benefits if they work better. This is why the focus of this conversation is to find opportunities for improvement, no matter how small. All ideas are valid.

2. Capture thoughts on content

Explain the different perspectives you are going to ask them to reflect on - content and process.

For content, ask them to reflect on the results achieved and to note down each of their thoughts on an individual post-it. If they do this individually first, it helps to reveal all ideas without the influence of "group think" and also to see how aligned the team members are in their thinking.

These are the questions they need to reflect on:

- What went well?
- What could have been better?
- What learning have they gained from working on them?

Once they have these, ask them to put them on the wall and group similar ones together.

Promote a discussion on the main points which are coming through and encourage them to draw conclusions and agree on actions—worth capturing these on a flip chart.

3. Capture thoughts on the process

Talk everyone through the Retro matrix you've put on the wall (or on a shared doc).

As per the last step, ask them to write down their individual thoughts on separate post-its in relation to the 3 questions against each of the 5 skill areas.

Once they have done this, ask them to group similar thoughts together, so there's some structure to what's being suggested.

Promote a discussion on the main points which are coming through and encourage them to draw conclusions and agree on actions. Don't forget to note these on a flip chart.

4. Wrap up

You should now have maybe a couple of flip chart sheets with actions. Make sure they have owners and time scales against them, and then check in that everyone is happy with the outputs from the Retro.

Transitions Between Cycles

I've seen it time and time again. Teams can become so focussed on delivering against their current OKRs, that they overlook preparing for the next quarter.

It's easily done, and this is why it needs the resident OKR Coach(es) to help teams remain on track with a clear timeline and the support they need to hit it.

What're the implications if this doesn't happen?

You will lose time out of your new quarter.

Arriving at the start of a new quarter with no OKRs already drafted means you'll need longer to prepare them, and you'll have less "uptime" to work on them once they are live.

We're not about to present you with a definitive blueprint of the perfect steps and timings - much will depend on what routines and processes you have in place already and how they can be adapted.

What you will learn, though, is the best sequence in which to approach it.

Recommended Timeline

Below are the week-by-week activities I find work well when managing the transition activity:

Week - 4

Exec/C-level assess likely to finish for the current quarter

- Using OKR confidence and progress data, a judgement is made as to where the current quarters OKRs are likely to finish
- Level 2 (quarterly) Objective Leads should be included in this discussion
- The prediction is mapped onto the Level 1 (annual) OKRs to judge the impact this quarter's progress will have on them

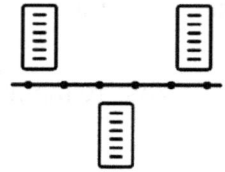

Reconfirm priorities for next quarter

- Now the anticipated impact on the Level 1 OKRs is clear, the priorities for the next quarter can be shared to help teams draft their Level 2 OKRs

Week - 3

Priorities for next quarter shared

- C-level & Objective Leads share what they predict will need to be the priorities for the next quarter

- If new cross-functional teams are required, this is the point at which they should be formed

Work starts on drafting the Level2 OKRs

- Level 2 OKRs are quarterly and are mainly worked on by cross-functional teams
- The teams work through ideas - both for new OKRs and next-stage development of existing ones

Week -2

Level 2 OKRs are shared

- It is valuable for teams to "test" their OKRs with other teams to make sure they stack up:
  o Do they make sense?
  o Is the alignment clear?
  o What are the dependencies & risks?

- If Level 3 OKRs are needed, then once the Level 2's are defined, they need to be presented to those who will be working on the Level 3's to ensure they are fully understood

Work starts on drafting Level 3 OKRs (if needed)

- Level 3 OKRs are typically quarterly and can be used to help align functional teams into a Level 2 OKR

- The teams who need to align into the Level 2 OKRs draft up their Level 3 OKRs

Week -1

Final "testing" of Level 2 & 3 OKRs

- See how closely the Level 3's align with the Level 2's
- It's likely that this final week will be very busy with a final push on the current OKRs, so don't expect too much time from teams here

Previous quarter closed off & Retro

- All OKR teams finalise the finish for their OKRs and run a Retrospective to capture learning from their progress and their use of OKRs
- Any recommendations for revising the use of OKRs are fed back to OKR Coaches for wider consideration

Analysis of finish against forecast

- C-level/Exec & OKR Leads assess the finish against what they forecasted
- C-level/Exec update Level 1 OKRs to reflect progress made in the previous quarter

Adjustments made

- Revisions are made to the draft OKRs if necessary
- This should be done in collaboration with OKR Leads and Key Contributors - NOT just changed by C-Level/Exec and then cascaded, or all the value gained from collaborating on the draft OKRs will be wasted

Show & Tell ceremony

- OKR Coaches facilitate
- Shows how all the OKRs align and checks for any risks/dependencies missed so they can be surfaced, and resolutions agreed
- OKR calendar for next quarter is shared

New OKRs go live

- OKRs go live on the system, and the cadence re-starts

Town Hall/All Hands update to the wider business

- A general update is done to the whole of the business, highlighting and giving recognition for major achievements, being transparent about misses, the major learning points and how they are influencing what comes next

How you can help as OKR Coach

As the OKR Coach, it's down to you to keep the OKR teams on track as they move through this period. Below are 3 things you can do to help them:

Publish a calendar for the quarter

It's rarely the case that months (and therefore quarters) start and finish at the beginning and end of a week. It's vital that a calendar is published, so teams understand the cadence they need to keep and key dates like when to start planning for the next quarter.

Friendly nudges

A nudge here and there is useful to help them stay on track once the calendar has been published, especially in the early stages of OKRs.

Facilitate

Especially in the early days of OKRs, confidence levels can get in the way of teams keeping to the cadence, so offering to facilitate to get the ball rolling is useful. You will also need to facilitate the larger ceremonies when planning starts for the next quarter.

Transitioning Into a New Year

If you're in Q4 and need to plan for the start of a new year, then there are a few differences we'd recommend as you help the organisation and teams prepare.

First of all, the strategic planning cycle of the organisation you're working in/with needs to be born in mind. It's highly like that work will start earlier planning for the next year than Q4; most C-level/Exec teams will kick this off in Q3.

Once the priorities for the coming year are clear, then it's the activities in Week -4 that need to flex a little and possibly even run a little earlier in the quarter.

Assessing the likely finish for the quarter & year

This shouldn't be too different in approach to the regular quarterly activity, which does this if the Level 1 OKRs have been updated after the end of each quarter. The principle difference is that the finish is both for the quarter and the year, which has strategic significance for the defining of annual priorities. These then need to be defined as Level 1 Objectives and, if Key Contributors have been involved, then also Key Results too.

Sharing priorities for next year

As we are looking at the full year ahead and not just the next quarter, it is worth allowing more time for the sharing and discussion of priorities (and possibly Level 1 OKRs) so people and teams can digest and fully understand the focus, the 'why' and start to think about what their contributions could be.

Final Thoughts and Next Steps

I really hope that you have found this to be a useful guide. I've aimed for it to be as practical and accessible as possible. There are deliberately no anecdotes, case studies or stories as I wanted it to be both brief and empirical. If you would like to hear first-hand how organisations have used OKRs, then tune in to our podcast, "Giant Talk" via your preferred platform or via www.therebegiants.com/podcast where you will find up to 100 interviews and discussions on the use of OKRs along with a practical audible OKR tool kit which makes a great companion to this Handbook.

If you are part of a cohort working through the OKR Coach Academy, then chances are we will have talked through your options. Hopefully, you will be joining our OKR Practitioner Community and working through to full Accreditation.

If you are using this Handbook and trying to work OKRs out for yourself, then don't worry - you are not alone! There are a few things you might want to check out:

OKR Coach Academy

I know I've mentioned it already, but as an overview, there are 3 levels to it:

OKR Activator - 100% e-learning. For individuals wanting to learn OKRs.

OKR Coach - blended e-learning & zoom workshops. For people aspiring to coach teams on OKRs.

OKR Master - blended e-learning & zoom workshops. For people aspiring to lead OKRs in an organisation.

Go to www.okrcoach.academy to access Activator or register your interest in Coach & Master.

I hope you have found this a useful guide and happy travels in the world of OKRs!